I WANT TO BE AN
ARTIST

Written by
Jonathan Reule

Illustration
Caballero Peza Mauricio
&
Caballero Peza Gabriel Fernando

Storyboard
Christiane Tee

First paperback edition March 2023
ISBN 978-981-18-6526-8

Published by Unibino Pte. Ltd.
31 Rochester Drive Level 3, #03-47 Singapore 138637

www.unibino.com

The world of art is vibrant and constantly changing. There are many artists in our modern world who contribute to making our society a beautiful place to live.

Do you enjoy drawing? Making clay figures? Or painting lovely landscapes? If that's the case, then maybe pursuing a career in art is the right path for you.

Before you do that, let's take a look at the history of art to better understand why we appreciate it so much! Did you know that the oldest piece of artwork found was a carving made from deer bones that are estimated to be around 51,000 years old?

What's even more interesting about this ancient work of art is that scholars are not entirely certain why the artist made it, which led to many different theories. Archaeologist Thomas Terberger mentioned in an interview that it was the start of culture, abstract thinking, and the birth of art. Perhaps creating beautiful works of art has always been in our DNA since the dawn of mankind.

Why do we love art so much? One reason is that many ancient civilisations had no form of written language, so they often recorded information and events through painting, carving, or sculpting.

Another reason is that some people believe that certain pieces of art are considered talismans or good luck charms. The Venus figurine is a statuette of a woman with a small head and large body which can be found throughout Europe.

Could this statue have represented the ability to birth many children? Or perhaps to have more than enough food to eat? Either way, the owner likely treasured this piece for the fortunes it might bring.

Other more advanced civilisations, such as the people of Mesopotamia, Egypt, Persia, and the Indus Valley, used art to spread religious or spiritual messages to the public. If you take a look at ancient temples that are still standing today, you'll see the hard work of many ancient artists!

Spirituality and religion were important parts of life in these civilisations of the past, and this can be seen through the beautiful temples that were built. Even to this day, places of worship are often beautifully decorated with intricate artwork and designs. How many artists do you think were involved when making such detailed temples as these?

As you can see, we found it easier to tell stories or record instructions through art pieces rather than written text. These artworks of the past capture the essence of their mythology and serve as constant reminders of those lessons.

That said, there are also many instances where artwork was used together with text to bring stories to life. The Code of Hammurabi is one of the oldest and most influential written laws inscribed on a 2.25 metres tall pillar, and the image of King Hammurabi is carved at the top to complement the Sumerian text inscribed onto it. Having the image of Hammurabi carved above the text makes the laws a bit more impactful!

The classical era was a period where humans experienced more prosperity and had time to create more beautiful art. The ancient Greeks were known for making magnificent statues of their gods, many of them even carved out of marble!

Rather than settling for simple carvings in temples or two-dimensional drawings, the Greeks wanted their gods to look and feel more realistic. Thus, the Greek craftsmen challenged themselves to make their sculptures as life-like as possible, and it seemed as if their artwork came to life!

During medieval times, artists started painting characters in a more realistic style with a background of large sprawling scenes to capture snapshots of full moments.

Art became more dynamic, detailed, and expressive. Artists also started painting a more accurate depiction of what they experienced. After the fall of the Roman empire, darker paintings with sadder tones became quite a popular style.

As art is often used as a medium of expression, it can help the artist convey all sorts of emotions. If the artist is experiencing sadness in their everyday life, it is likely that this underlying emotion can be felt through their work. Being an artist is more than just knowing how to paint, carve, or sculpt. One must also have a keen sense of observation.

During the Renaissance period when times were not so tough, intellectual pursuits began to flourish again. The prevalent art style of this period had brighter scenes, and many iconic pieces of work that we all know and love were created during this time as well!

Most artists are able to see the world with a unique or different perspective than other people. Even though a particular style may be popular for a period of time, it does not mean it will stay that way. What is now known as modern art was birthed not long after the Renaissance period.

This was a period when artists were experimenting with new and unique styles. Some artists played with shapes in both paintings and sculptures, while others depicted people with exaggerated facial expressions or poses to create a more striking piece. In general, these artists were willing to try new techniques and styles, and many of the artists and their artwork eventually became well-known names in history.

After the Modern period is the period of contemporary art. Over the past few decades, there were many innovations in the way artists created and presented art. From animated cartoons to corporate logos for companies and even abstract pieces, artists have never stopped reinventing and experimenting with how they express themselves.

This period also coincided with the invention of personal computers, and as technology became more advanced, artists started to create digital art. If you have ever watched a digital animation either in the cinema or on your computer, remember that it takes several skilled digital artists to draw those scenes and make them move!

In many ways, digitalisation had a significant impact on contemporary artwork. With the help of computers, artists could work much faster and more efficiently. They could now have all the colour palettes and patterns they want at their fingertips, as well as keep their work safe and organised in case they need to return to it later for touch-ups!

This is why it is important for budding artists to be familiar with the different tools and applications that are available to them. For many professional fields such as graphic design, interior design, and even digital animation, knowing how to use graphic manipulation software is essential. However, these digital programmes will not be able to do everything for you! You will still need to work on your skill.

Now that you have a better understanding of art — how it began and why humans have been creating art for thousands of years — you will need to decide if you would like to be a part of this diverse field.

If you want to be an artist, you will need to take the first step – just start creating! First, find a style or medium that you enjoy. There are many to choose from, such as digital drawing, sculpting, watercolour painting, charcoal sketching, and so much more. Daily practice will give you the best foundation you need.

After that, you can consider attending a specialised art school or a fine arts course where you can hone in on your craft and meet other inspiring artists just like yourself. This can be a great way to find out what your peers are doing, learn from your teachers, and you can then narrow in on your own artistic niche.

Or, if you prefer to take another route, you could always try to secure a mentorship with an established artist who can give you the guidance you need to break into the field of art. Doing this can also be a great way to learn faster, especially since you will be gaining practical experience while working for your mentor.

There are many artists who do not desire to sell their works or even work for a big company. For such artists, there are still other options to explore where they can apply their artistic talents. Being an art teacher allows artists to instruct eager learners with the knowledge and skills they have acquired and still be able to make a living in a field that they love.

Art directors are often professional artists who join teams of artists who are all working on the same project. For example, an art director with a video game company oversees the designs of the game, from the game characters to backgrounds, and even items within the world.

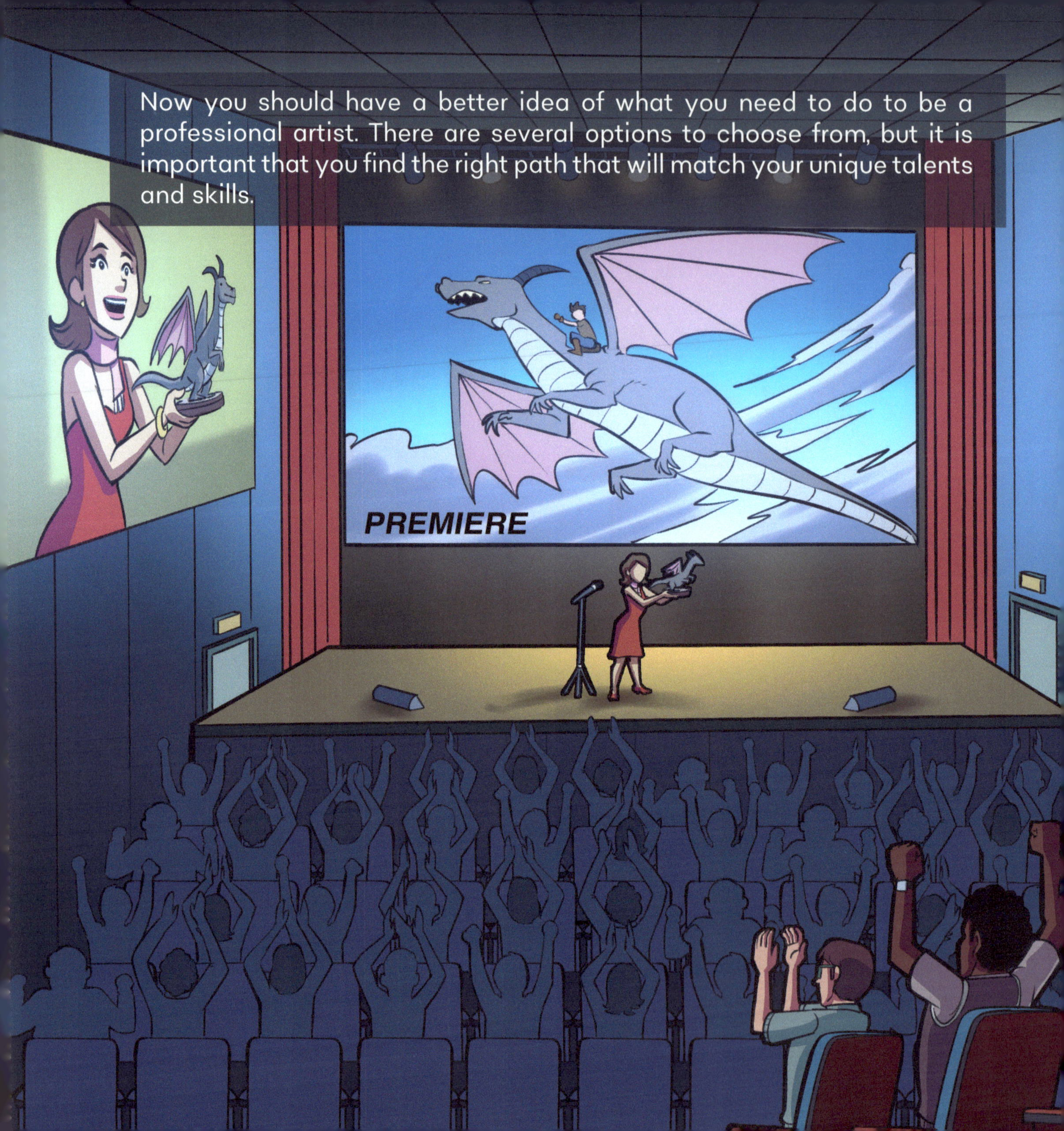

Now you should have a better idea of what you need to do to be a professional artist. There are several options to choose from, but it is important that you find the right path that will match your unique talents and skills.

Who knows, maybe you will be a well-known artist or you may work for an animation company that entertains millions of people. But no matter what you decide, it is important that you keep your passion for creating art in your heart. As art is a medium of expression, how you feel will ultimately shine through your work.

My Inspiration

Shubhi Saxena
Founder, Unibino

As a parent in this ever-changing world, it can sometimes feel overwhelming when it comes to our children's futures. New technologies seem to be arising almost every day, and with so many innovations, it creates unique professions which many of us wouldn't have dreamed to be necessary only a few years ago. Which to me is a good thing. Because with so much variety, my children can have the opportunity to pick a career that will fit their personalities and build upon their strengths. As you may imagine, this desire within me to provide my children with the resources they needed to thrive, led me to search out books that would be easy enough for them to understand while teaching them about various professions.

Only, I found that these books were few and far between. Even if I could find a book about a certain profession geared towards young readers, I found them sparse inside and limited to only certain careers that may not fit my children's abilities. This is when I came up with the idea to write my own children's books, teaching them about all the various careers in the modern world. After months of researching different professions and learning more than I ever expected, I quickly realised this was going to be a bigger project than I first anticipated. I dove into the histories of these professions, discovering links to the past, and why these professions were now so important.

Ultimately my goal was to offer my children options, to show them that there is no one set path for everyone. But in this, I stumbled upon something bigger. I wanted to share this with future generations. To share with all children and parents about these careers, to help spark curiosity, and to instil a passion for the future. Everyone has special talents and abilities, and I hope that this series will be able to offer clarity and inspiration to children around the world. Because at the end of the day, it's never too early to start dreaming and never too late to take action. With this, I hope you enjoy this series and that your young ones become the best versions of themselves as they can achieve.